The Habits of Highly Joyful People

Penetrate the Secrets of Profound Happiness With This Little Book

Inspirational Creator

ISBN 978-1-922940-22-3 (E-book)

ISBN 978-1-922940-25-4 (Paperback)

Cover Design by Liam Daniels

Published by Inspirational Creator

Liam Daniels

First Edition (2023)

Table of Contents

Introduction

People everywhere, and always, have sought the key to happiness. –Tal Ben-Shahar

Finding happiness is our greatest preoccupation in life. Everything we do—getting a job, making money, seeking friendship, building a family, achieving victories—we do because we want to be happy. In fact, happiness is so important that we often use the concept interchangeably with finding meaning in life or fulfilling a purpose.

But the truth is that we don't often stop to evaluate the meaning behind everything we do. Caught up in the hustle and bustle of everyday life, we rarely question if what we are doing is what truly matters for a meaningful life. Others wait patiently for something to happen so that they can finally be happy, but little do they know that this philosophy will only push them into an eternal cycle of seeking but never finding happiness.

So, what is happiness? Despite most people having experienced it in their lives, happiness is notoriously hard to define. This is because it is intrinsically subjective, and in fact, the preferred term for happiness in positive psychology is "subjective well-being." That's one definition in itself. Another good one is: “A state characterized by contentment and general satisfaction with one’s current situation” (Ackerman, 2019).

Others may have different definitions of happiness that hold more meaning to them—be it poetic, spiritual, or religious—but for the purposes of this book, a more scientific approach will be taken.

Ongoing research has given us invaluable insights into the study of happiness. I will reference several different studies and findings from a variety of fields, such as positive psychology, behavioral science, and life coaching. Through close observation of the minds of others, they have revealed remarkable—and sometimes surprising—truths about the human condition of happiness. In some areas, I have also drawn on anecdotes from my own personal journey with happiness.

All this being said, we can never fully understand someone else’s mind or their subjective experience, and so we must accept that there will always be an element to happiness that evades explanation.

So, where does joy come in? And how is it different from happiness? Generally, joy is described as an intense feeling of pleasure and delight that arises in the present moment. So, while happiness can be a long-term state, joy is more of a fleeting emotion. Joy is also something that we feel for, and in response to, other people, whereas happiness is more often concerned with the self. Joy is also an emotion that can share space with others, like sadness, doubt, or anger. It can convert heartache into gratitude and darkness into hope. Choosing joy is often the first step toward becoming a happier, more positive person.

Happiness is not a new preoccupation. Over 2,500 years ago, Plato formulated his philosophy of "the good life" in ancient Greece, as was Confucius in ancient China. And this is only what we have a physical record of; we can be sure the pursuit of happiness was going on long before we invented writing.

Today, happiness is commodified and obsessed over by modern society. Social media, consumer goods companies, and entertainment giants inundate us with images and stories of "happy people," i.e., individuals more talented, more successful, and better-looking than us. We buy into this illusion that if we're not happy, there's something wrong with us. But these industries that supposedly promote happiness are the very channels through which toxic mentalities are spread. Doesn't all this seem contradictory? It is no wonder that anxiety and depression rates are at an all-time high, especially among young people. The good news is this doesn't have to be your reality.

What distinguishes humans from all other animals is our inherent ability to take ownership of our life. Once you realize this, happiness becomes a real possibility and not just a question of winning the lottery. Research has shown that our overall life satisfaction is influenced by 50% genetics, 10% external factors, and 40% individual actions (Lyubomirsky, Sheldon, Schkade, 2005). So, even if your genetics are against you, you have the power to make your life a happy one.

This book aims to give you a deeper and more helpful understanding of happiness. It will teach you ways to become happier and break down some common myths and misconceptions about happiness and how to achieve it. Please note, merely reading this book is not going to fix your problems or change your life. As happiness expert Tal Ben-Shahar notes, "There are no shortcuts to meaningful change" (Ben-Shahar, 2007).

For this book to make a real difference in your life, you must reflect on the ideas that you read and take meaningful action. You will encounter some exercises throughout the book that will help you with this. Treat them as a start to implementing positive practices in your life. It is my hope that, after finishing this book, you will have a clearer idea of what you need to do to become a happier person. At the very least, you will know the right questions to ask yourself, questions that will ultimately lead you down the path to joy and happiness.

Before moving on to the next chapter, I invite you to think about what happiness means to you. What comes into your mind? What associations, definitions, or requirements pop up? Write down your thoughts, being completely honest with yourself. Don't worry about presenting them in a coherent manner at this point, but make sure you keep these ideas—you will be revisiting them at the end.

Chapter 1: Are We Innately Happy?

The greatest joys in life are happy memories, which you can revisit at any moment of time. Therefore, the great business of life is to create as many of them as possible. –Michel de Montaigne

We readily accept that suffering is a part of life, a necessity even. We brace ourselves for an abundance of it. Happiness, on the other hand, is often viewed as something that some people have, and others don't—and which category you find yourself in is mostly down to luck and circumstance.

This binary response is aggravated by the very question, "Am I happy?" It limits the options to: "Yes, I'm happy." or "No, I'm not." But happiness is not an endpoint, it is a continuum. Trying to reach it as if it were a final destination will only bring you frustration and disappointment.

Perhaps a more helpful question would be, "How can I enjoy the process more from this moment onward?" This immediately removes the impossible task of trying to quantify happiness and instead encourages you to focus on the ongoing—and lifelong—process of becoming happier. Because happiness is actually the default human nature, not suffering. It is not something you save up for or work towards. Why? Because you already have it. You've always had it. It dwells within you.

This is the central teaching of Srikumar Rao, an elite coach of personal growth and transformation. He believes that all humans are innately happy, that we are born with happiness "hard-wired" into us. To become happier, therefore, all we have to do is tap into our abundant natural resources.

In order to do this, we must first unlearn a dominant mental model in our society, sometimes referred to as the "If/Then" model. It follows a formula of, "If/when X happens, then I will be happy/happier." For example, "If I buy a new car, then I will be much happier." or "If I marry a beautiful woman, then I will be happy," which basically means, "I won't be happy until I find someone." We tell ourselves that, first, we must *get* something in order to *do* something so that we can *be* someone. Only then will we be happy.

We have invested so completely in this model that we frequently mistake it for the truth. This is deeply problematic because, in actuality, it is a heavily flawed model fueled by consumerism. It leads us to believe that happiness resides in the end goal; we cannot be happy until we have reached it. But if your happiness depends on one particular outcome, you are bound to fail because outcomes are completely out of your control. Plus, there is no guarantee that this outcome will bring the happiness that it promises. In the best case, it may bring euphoria, but certainly not lasting happiness.

Focusing on the outcome also means you can't enjoy the present because you're constantly caught up in the future. You are dragged into a cycle of always thinking about the next step; a promotion, a pay rise, a bigger house. This is unanimously advised against by happiness experts because it essentially means delaying happiness and missing out on living. Doing this means you will never be truly happy, and by the time you realize this, it may be too late. We only get one life, and tomorrow isn't promised.

It is often the people who enter into this "rat race" that protest when speakers like Rao announce that happiness is our innate nature. They say to themselves, "If happiness is hard-wired into us, then why am I not happy?" "Why have I never been happy?" "Why can't I feel happy, no matter how hard I try?" The answer is probably that they have invested in a flawed mental model and have been delaying and denying themselves happiness from the start.

So, what's the solution? Unlearning such a deeply ingrained model is not easy. Pretty much all happiness experts agree that the first step is to stop focusing on the outcome and invest in the process instead. The decisions and actions you take during the process are much more within your control than the outcome. And humans need control to be happy. Try to make the process so enjoyable that, even if the final outcome is lacking, it was still worth it.

This brings us to the second step; being in the present moment. Feelings of anxiety have been linked to how we perceive the future, while depression has often been associated with how we make sense of the past. These are the enemies of inner peace. The only way to true happiness is to be in the present and to accept life as it is. Do not allow yourself to be disturbed by the unfortunate or uncontrolled aspects of life.

To emphasize this point further, think of a time when you truly marveled at something. When you had a sight before you, that evoked a deep sense of serenity and awe. A mountain range, perhaps, or the sun setting over the ocean. Or maybe it's the first time you saw your newborn's face. Most people will have at least one memory like this. And what do all of these beautiful memories have in common? They occurred when you were in the present.

People who are truly happy, then, are not so because they had lucky genetics or were born into a life of privilege. They are happy because they can take pleasure in whatever's right in front of them. They find joy in the present moment, in daily life experiences, and in the little things life has to offer. They don't need to wait for the next best thing because they understand that they are able to feel joy now. This happiness is just as available to you as it is to them. But if you live in the future waiting for X to happen or in the past, which you cannot change or control, you will fail to appreciate the present, and your pursuit of happiness will be a perpetual one.

Chapter 2: What You Should Prioritize Most

The greatest wealth is health. –Virgil

Health and happiness are inextricably intertwined. We've all heard the cliché, "Your body is your temple," but it is a simple fact that your mind and body cannot serve you well if you don't treat them respectfully. You will never be able to reach your full potential if you lack good health. It elevates your mood and enriches your body—from your skin and hair to every internal organ and system you have. And, of course, being healthy allows you to live a longer, happier life. Therefore, whatever situation you are in, you must do everything in your power to prioritize your health—which is, in essence, you.

Please note: This is not a book about optimizing your health—such a vast topic would warrant a whole book in itself. Its inclusion here is simply to give you an overview of the best practices for looking after your mental and physical health and how they impact your happiness. I would encourage you to do some of your own research as well. Each person's health needs are specific and personal to them, and there is lots of information out there that can benefit you.

Nourishment

It's hard to overstate how important it is to eat and drink well. The idea that what we eat affects our physical health has long been established, but with the emerging field of nutritional psychiatry, researchers are drawing direct links between food and mental health as well. For example, we now have a much better idea about the remarkable system of communication between the gut and the brain. When we eat healthy food, we promote a healthy gut. The gut then produces compounds like dopamine and serotonin, signaling to the brain to release them into our body and regulate our moods and emotions.

Therefore, people who maintain a balanced diet generally enjoy greater well-being and lead happier lives. Foods that are rich in antioxidants are particularly beneficial. For instance, studies have shown that simply eating three or more pieces of fruit and vegetables per day leads to higher levels of optimism and reduced levels of depression, anxiety, and stress. There are many other nutrient-rich options out there—some better for you than others—hence the importance of expanding your knowledge on it. When it comes to happiness, food can be a wonderful and empowering resource.

Of course, it can also work the other way, and some food and drink will have the opposite effect on your body. As much as possible, avoid processed food and products pumped full of sugar and salt. They also have a higher risk of containing microplastics. Be mindful of the effects of excessive drinking and smoking. These actions may be normalized by society, but both alcohol and nicotine are depressants that chemically tamper with your brain and ultimately prevent you from being happy.

Take the time to research food and drink that is healthy for your brain and the body. It is also important to educate yourself on the effects the food industry has on the world. For example, the rising levels of microplastics in the ocean affect sea life and end up in our seafood. The use of pesticides in farming and other contaminants like heavy metals in the food we buy. What affects the natural world inevitably affects us. It could be the reason why we have seen an increase in health conditions such as autoimmune diseases in the last couple of decades.

Be mindful of how much meat you are eating, and perhaps consider experimenting with a more plant-based diet. You could even get creative and set yourself challenges, such as cooking one new recipe each week or trying food from different cultures. If culinary exploration isn't your thing, team up with a friend or relative who loves to cook and strike a deal; you supply them with an exotic superfood, and they build a recipe around it!

Finally, be sure to drink plenty of water. Doctors advise that adult females should be drinking 2.7 liters of water each day, and adult males should be drinking 3.7 liters. If you're someone who forgets to drink water, try filling up a couple of 1-liter bottles at the beginning of the day. Leave them out on the counter or on your desk so that you're constantly reminded to drink.

Exercise

Regular exercise is crucial to maintaining good physical and mental health. It is a major antidepressant and yet is the least utilized. Exercising is advice you will see come up again and again from all corners. Not only does it release the "happy hormones" (dopamine and serotonin), but it also teaches your brain that your behavior has consequences, both positive and negative. What we do matters.

This does not mean you have to drag yourself to the gym three times a week and make yourself miserable. There are many ways to exercise. For example, you could join your local football club or go to tennis lessons with a friend. Both options also have an added social benefit. Perhaps sport isn't your thing, but you're a dance lover or yoga enthusiast. Anything that gets you moving is beneficial.

Walking can be an excellent option, too, and should never be underestimated. It has a vast array of physical health benefits; improved cardiovascular and pulmonary fitness, reduced body fat, stronger muscles, better balance and endurance, lower risk of heart disease, diabetes, cancer, and many more. Walking also has a marked effect on your mental health, particularly if it entails being immersed in nature or in the company of a loved one, both of which are very soothing and de-stressing. Walking offers the mind a chance to relax and clear, to organize and rationalize, and sometimes to switch off completely. Many great artists, poets, writers, and thinkers have sworn that their greatest ideas came to them whilst walking.

Sleep

Sleep and health have a close relationship. With enough sleep, your body can function normally, and your well-being is enhanced. Sleep deprivation, on the other hand, is disabling and dims the quality of your life in every way. It can lead to a whole range of mental consequences, from irritability and stress to chronic depression and psychosis. The physical side effects are just as varied and severe.

The problem is, when we don't get enough sleep, we start worrying and worrying makes it harder to fall asleep. The two become caught up in a vicious cycle. It is thus imperative to get a handle on your routine and build good sleeping habits. This might include doing the following:

- As much as possible, go to bed and wake up at the same time each day to regulate your body clock.
- Turn off all screens and electronics an hour before you go to sleep.
- Invest in a good mattress and good-quality sheets.
- If necessary, buy blackout blinds.

- Do not eat dinner too late, and do not drink alcohol or caffeine before sleeping.
- Get plenty of physical exercise, but no later than three hours before bedtime.
- Set the right room temperature (typically a bit cooler for sleeping).
- Consider using air plugs.

If your work or lifestyle doesn't follow the standard nine-to-five routine, it doesn't matter as long as you can find a pattern that works for you. In his research into sleep, Matthew Walker talks about how some of us are "morning larks" and others "night owls." The former make up around 40% of the population and tend to reach peak wakefulness in the morning. Another 30% of the population are night owls, who reach this peak in the evening instead. This is due to a difference in their circadian rhythms.

Humans developed this difference as a means of survival. Having a mixture of morningness chronotypes and eveningness chronotypes ensured an almost constant 24-hour watch against predators. Morning larks would go to sleep early while the night owls stayed up. The night owls would then go to sleep just a few hours before the morning larks woke up, reducing the window of night exposure to 2–3 hours instead of 6–8 hours. This also facilitated short-term mating.

From an evolutionary standpoint, then, each chronotype is as necessary as the other; night owls, morning larks, and everyone in between. In the world today, night owls are often put at a disadvantage due to societal biases. If you are more of a night owl and work better in the evening or at night, do not feel ashamed. It is simply because your biological clock is set to a later hour. Spend some time looking into which circadian rhythm is best attuned to you and build a routine around it.

Mental Health

The road to better mental health starts with self-care. Self-care is a vast umbrella term for lots of different things, and everything already mentioned can come under it. For me, it is principally about love, self-compassion, and acceptance. If you can achieve this, you can extend it to other people. Exactly how you go about this will be personal to you, but there are steps we can take as a community to make it easier for everyone.

First, we can all work towards de-stigmatizing mental health. Although it is talked about more openly than ever, mental health is still surrounded by judgment and distaste. Take the time to educate yourself on the signs and symptoms of mental illness—not just for yourself but so you can identify it in others too. Talk about your feelings with people you trust, and never be afraid to seek help if you need it. Remember, good mental health is not just the absence of illness. It is the active engagement with positivity and happiness.

Second, find a healthy work-life balance. This is vitally important to your health and happiness, and we will be discussing it in more depth in the next chapter. Think about how you divide your time between work and leisure. Are you satisfied with the way you're currently balancing things? Keep a lookout for burnout alerts such as fatigue, headaches, anxiety, feeling drained, and having an increasingly helpless or cynical outlook on life. Knowing the signs can help you prevent a breakdown. And finally, make sure you're getting plenty of rest and relaxation. You could even treat yourself to a spa day or massage!

Third, pay attention to your thoughts and do not ignore your intuition. Be mindful of what you dislike or are not comfortable with. Set boundaries for yourself in regard to other people, i.e., learn how to say no when it matters. This can be difficult to practice as we naturally want to help people, but at some point, you must draw the line and stop living to please others. Taking the "politely assertive" route is usually the best bet. Furthermore, listen to your hopes and desires. To do this is to listen to yourself. It will help you cope with stress and keep peace of mind. And, of course, do not forget to set aside time to have fun, share a joke with someone, or simply just to smile.

This leads me to a final point here. Positive thinking. This may sound obvious, but it is remarkable how conditioned we are to look for faults instead of benefits. Try to infuse your life with optimism wherever possible. Not only will it make you feel better about yourself, but it will also improve your creativity and productivity. It can be a win-win or a lose-lose situation.

Positive thinking should extend to how you treat others as well. Practice being kind and compassionate and let go of negative feelings such as hatred, jealousy, guilt, and regret. These emotions are hugely damaging and never do anyone any good. In fact, research has shown that people who practice forgiveness enjoy better mental health and higher levels of life satisfaction.

Chapter 3: Managing your Time

"Count your age by friends, not years. Count your life by smiles, not tears." –John Lennon

Time is our most valuable non-renewable resource. It has the ability to give you everything but also the power to take away just as much. It is no surprise, then, that time well-managed has a direct correlation to happiness, and time wasted or neglected increases the chances of feeling miserable and depressed. Learning how to use your time wisely and carefully will open you up to higher levels of productivity and creativity and give you the opportunity to focus on the people and things you love.

One of the most effective ways to manage your time is to get a handle on your habits. Our brains use habits to automate as much behavior as possible so as to free up space in the conscious mind to focus on other tasks. While this can be a very useful strategy, it also means that bad habits are automated. And bad habits have a tendency to eat up time.

For example, if you have a habit of drinking too much on the weekends, you will waste all of your free time in bed with a hangover. Conversely, if you have a habit of washing up in the evening and laying your briefcase out, you will have more time to read or share breakfast with someone the next morning.

The best advice I've come across for building a good habit is James Clear's technique of starting with small, 1% improvements each day and slowly building them up. Focus on repetition, not perfection—even two minutes of dedication are better than none. If you're struggling to stick to a new habit, get really specific with the time and place where you'll perform it. Maybe even attach it to a habit that you already do regularly to make it easier to remember. Give yourself rewards for completing the habit to make it more attractive, and if you slip up and miss a day, make sure you get back on track as quickly as possible.

The idea is to make those positive new habits as easy to implement as possible. When it comes to breaking a bad habit, you have to do the opposite. Remove any visual cues in your environment that might trigger a bad habit, such as your phone, your Xbox, or the jar of cookies in the kitchen. Make the consequences of performing a bad habit immediately painful so that your brain is less likely to repeat it. Remind yourself of the most important thing you have to gain from avoiding a bad habit: Time.

Another obstacle to optimizing your time is procrastination. We are all guilty of procrastinating once in a while. The trick is to notice *when* you are procrastinating and *why*. You can then employ the appropriate strategies needed to overcome it. For instance, if you're procrastinating because you're disorganized, make a to-do list and prioritize it in terms of urgency. Alternatively, if you're procrastinating because the task is overwhelming or difficult, pick a time of the day when you're most productive. Break the task down into more manageable chunks and work in short bursts with regular breaks. Beating procrastination is like breaking a bad habit; it requires patience and determination.

As you get your habits in shape and your day-to-day starts to become more organized, you'll find you have more free time to focus on your well-being and savor life. If you're unsure about what makes you happy, experiment with a wide range of different hobbies and activities or even get to know new people to spend time with.

It should get to a point where you're spending 80–90% of your free time enjoying activities that you get the most out of and 10–20% exploring other projects. This concept, known as the "explore/exploit trade-off" (Clear, 2018), is an excellent way to avoid wasting time on things that don't stimulate you and to focus on the things you are passionate about instead. It is a cycle that encourages you to constantly improve through exploration and creativity.

The main takeaway is: Take time for yourself to discover what makes you feel good and fulfilled. In his seminal work, *The 4-Hour Workweek*, Tim Ferriss takes this approach to the extreme with his "mini-retirements" philosophy (Ferriss, 2007). This is the idea of taking regular breaks throughout your working life to relocate or travel. It could be for one week, one month, or even six months. The point that matters most here is taking time for yourself—the more you can spare, the better.

Why save all of your retirement time for the end? Why not enjoy it on a regular basis instead of spending your whole working life anticipating this "one-time event." In order to live life to the fullest and maximize your happiness, you must not fall into the mentality of waiting. Waiting the eight hours until your working day is done; waiting for the weekend; waiting for a vacation; waiting for retirement. As I mentioned in Chapter 1, all that means is your life will pass you by. Instead, shift your focus and commit to constantly looking for new ways to enjoy the process and be in the present moment. In other words, stop counting the hours and make them count instead.

If you hate your job—and there is no shame in that—you might need to make some important decisions, particularly if you suffer from going to work every single day. If your job is "okay," perhaps you want to reassess your priorities, such as reexamining how much time you devote to work. Especially following the 2020 pandemic, attitudes to work are shifting, and a more flexible, hybrid approach is becoming increasingly popular.

A four-day working week has already been trialed in many countries, with the latest in the UK being hailed as "a major breakthrough" (Joly & Hurst, 2023). In many countries, researchers found a decrease in stress and burnout among employees and an increase in their general well-being. As the work-life balance improved, productivity levels also went up.

Optimizing time is not just about personal time management, it's also about the time you give to others. This is arguably the most valuable gift you can give to someone, so it's crucial not to waste it on people who don't value you or appreciate you. Do not live your life to please others. Instead, spend quality time with the people that you love and trust. If you're not sure whether someone is a positive presence in your life or not, ask yourself, "Do I feel good about myself after hanging out with them?" We will cover this more in the next chapter.

Chapter 4: Why Relationships Matter

There isn't time, so brief is life, for bickerings, apologies, heartburnings, callings to account. There is only time for loving, and but an instant, so to speak, for that. –Mark Twain

At 115 years old, María Branyas Morera is the oldest woman in the world. When asked what her secret to longevity is, she replied, "Staying away from toxic people." This may sound overly simplistic, but the latest research shows that the people we surround ourselves with and the relationships we form with them—or don't—is the single most impactful factor on our health and happiness.

We have always known that humans are social creatures, and our need to seek approval and fit in with the tribe is a basic survival instinct. But recent insights from the Harvard Study of Adult Development have revealed just how crucial relationships are to a meaningful life. Championed as the longest-running study on happiness in the world, the Harvard study is an ongoing project that has been following the lives of original participants and their descendants since 1938. The most notable observation researchers have made is that the participants who are socially connected and enjoy loving relationships are the most content with their lives.

In other words, if you want a good life, you need good relationships. These relationships can take many different forms; family, friends, romantic partners, pets, colleagues, teachers, community members, and more. Researchers have also found that the quality of our relationships has a direct impact on our physical and mental health. Any positive social connection will contribute positively to your happiness.

On the other hand, study participants who were isolated and lonely experienced a faster decline in health than those who had loving, supportive relationships. They also died sooner. In fact, sufferers of chronic loneliness are 26% more likely to die in any given year of their lives (Waldinger and Schulz, 2023). Loneliness literally kills.

When asked about their biggest regrets in life, many of the older participants said it was not maintaining their relationships. Don't let this be you. Learn from the unprecedented insights that this study has to offer and start cultivating warm relationships today. It is possibly the most important choice you will ever make. Even if you feel you already have good relationships in your life, there is always room to improve.

Take a moment to reflect on how much time and attention you devote to different areas of your life. Do you spend a disproportionate amount of time doing one thing? A study from 2018 revealed that Americans spend eleven hours a day interacting with some form of media, be it television or radio, laptops or smartphones. Within the space of 40 years, that adds up to 18 years of living. Can you relate to this? If so, shifting your focus away from this area might be a good first step. Think about how much of that screen time could be spent seeing friends and family instead.

Of course, this is easier said than done. One reason why we neglect our social duties is because they take up so much time and effort and are not always rewarding. For this reason, it can sometimes help to approach a relationship as you would a new habit. Start small and do not overcomplicate it. Meaningful connections can be made through a simple phone call or a 10-minute walk.

Furthermore, accepting challenges is a necessary part of the process. Do not let them deter you, but rather be grateful for them. Navigating the complex and unpredictable nature of human connection is how we learn and grow. See each unfolding of a relationship as an opportunity and not a burden—

and take comfort in the fact that, when you get to the later years of your life, it will have been absolutely worth it. To love is the noblest of human pursuits, and for that reason, it gives the greatest benefit in return; true happiness.

It is never too late to forge new relationships or work on the ones you already have. I, therefore, want to end this chapter with a call to action. Think about a person in your life that you would like to connect with more. Invite them out for a hot drink. Simple gestures like this are a great way to start cultivating stronger relationships with people.

Chapter 5: Should Money Be on the List?

Happiness is not found in things you possess but in what you have the courage to release. – Nathaniel Hawthorne

Money first came into being to serve as a tool for humans to exchange their resources and support their communities. It was used at our convenience. Today, that control has switched, and money seems to hold sway over the majority of our decisions and actions. It has become the principal way in which we measure each other's worth and has grown so powerful that it can compromise even the most intrinsic of moral and ethical values.

Unsurprisingly, then, money has a complicated relationship with happiness. It can sometimes be the source of great joy and comfort, and other times the antithesis. The perennial question, "Can money buy happiness?" has been answered and interpreted from many different angles. The latest research suggests that yes, it can. To an extent. In the US, for example, studies show that happiness rises with annual income until it hits the $70–90,000 range, after which it doesn't seem to make so much of a difference (Suliman, 2023, Gilbert, 2007). By no means does this indicate that you need $70,000 to be happy (in the US), or any specific amount for that matter. For you, the income/happiness curve might flatten long before that figure, depending on your specific situation and needs, your personality, and many other factors.

In other words, rising from poverty to the middle class makes a big difference in people's happiness, but beyond that, it becomes less of a contributing factor. You could be earning $5 million per year and still be unlikely to be much happier than someone making $70,000. Money doesn't guarantee happiness, then, but it's certainly necessary for living a stable and comfortable life. Being financially impoverished can lead to difficult and sometimes even dangerous situations, where all the basics of life—food, water, shelter, healthcare—are no longer available to you. Without these, happiness is virtually impossible.

In some cases, impoverishment comes from a lack of understanding about money and how it works. This is why it's so important to have some sort of financial education. It allows you to use money with greater ease and confidence, and it gives you an advantage when navigating this money-driven world. Specifically, this means helping you to understand how inflation works, how it impacts your savings, how to prepare for each situation, what happens during the different economic cycles, what you should invest in and why, and so on. Like anything in life, the more educated you are on a topic, the more informed your choices will be.

Where it starts to go wrong is when people think money is the most important thing. They see it as a requisite for happiness and therefore spend most of their lives obsessively pursuing it. This gives way to a toxic mentality that encourages greed, entitlement, and exploitation. It is the reason why most of the world's wealth lies in the hands of a few, while so many go without the most fundamental of human needs. Because of this, many people have a negative view of money and see it as a corrupting force in the world.

Activist Lynne Twist explains our relationship with money through a dichotomy of mentalities: Scarcity and sufficiency (Twist, 2006). Those who buy into the mentality of scarcity are the ones who tell themselves they don't have enough money and that they need more to be happy. Many of us do this without even realizing it. Another symptom of the scarcity mindset is believing that there is nothing you can do to change the world's broken systems. You perceive yourself to be helpless and powerless and so enter into the system with the hope of coming out on top. Unfortunately, all this leads to a perpetual cycle of anguish and dread. You spend so much time and energy worrying about money that you don't make use of what you already have.

The sufficiency mentality, on the other hand, lies in the conviction that what you have is enough and there is no need to chase after what you don't really need. All that energy spent on worrying can now be directed toward making meaningful use of your resources. Twist uses the metaphor of water to powerfully communicate this idea further. When water moves or is given away, it supports life. When it stays still or is withheld, it stagnates. Money is exactly the same. It is supposed to flow, to be spent and shared, not saved and guarded. An unmoving pile of money doesn't serve anyone or any purpose.

If you want to be happier, let go of the scarcity mindset. Relax into the belief that there are enough resources for everyone and start contributing towards a world that shares them equally. Once we start practicing generosity, our happiness increases, and once we become happier, we are more motivated to be generous. It is a continuous positive cycle!

My personal philosophy towards money is that it should flow towards buying more time, either in the form of money or more time itself. All the while, I keep in mind the sufficiency mindset, taking care not to fall into fear or greed. Both time and money can be spent on the things you enjoy and the people you love. These are the things that matter to me, and as long as my money is an expression of those beliefs, I am happy.

In answer to this chapter's question, then, yes, money should be on the list. It should be included in the wider conversation about happiness. Not only because it is so misunderstood but also because it is an essential tool originally invented to facilitate the exchange and flow of resources. It should be returned to that original purpose. Once a healthy relationship has been reinstated, we might find money surprisingly conducive to inner peace and happiness.

Chapter 6: The Mindset of Joyful People

What lies before us and what lies behind us are small matters compared to what lies within us. And when we bring what is within out into the world, miracles happen. –Henry David Thoreau

A common misconception about happy people is that they are never sad. When we talk about being happy, what we often envisage is being happy *all* the time. But this is not the case, and happy people experience the full range of emotions just like everyone else. Yes, they tend to feel positive more often than they feel negative, but this is only because they are better at accepting and dealing with difficult emotions. Science tells us that a portion of our happiness is determined by genetics, but just because you weren't born with a natural advantage doesn't mean you can't be as happy as those who were. Being happy and joyful is all about mindset.

It all starts with accepting and loving yourself. If you hate yourself, this will conflict with any positive change you try to make. Practicing self-compassion will increase optimism and inner peace and advocate growth. For this reason, it is important to remember to treat yourself gently and kindly. Nurture that inner, vulnerable place like you would a child that you love. How we treat ourselves often mirrors our treatment of others, so being compassionate to yourself will also improve your relations with other people.

Having a positive mindset stems from emotional intelligence. This does not mean that happy people are smarter. It means they have learned to manage their own emotions and communicate empathetically with others. An important part of this process is acceptance. In meditation, we are taught to be more aware and to accept our thoughts, feelings, and emotions as they arise. We notice them, acknowledge them, and then gently guide our minds back to the practice.

Meditation can teach you how to move through these thoughts and emotions without feeling stuck, which eventually leads to you feeling better about yourself. Recognizing how you are feeling without judgment or extreme reaction creates a safe space for positive reflection and development.

In fact, research shows that pretending to be happy when you're not is actually harmful to your health. It places enormous pressure on your mind and body and sets unrealistic expectations. Furthermore, when you repress your emotions, all you are doing is leaving them unaddressed and unchecked. As a result, they do not go away but rather strengthen and threaten to burst out in uncontrolled ways. Happy people are not threatened by difficult emotions. They accept them as important signals or appropriate reactions to life. They deal with them while maintaining an underlying awareness that these feelings will pass, and things will get better.

Acceptance also means letting go of control. It means maintaining a positive outlook even when things don't go your way. This is easier said than done; the need for control is deeply embedded in human nature. Not only does it make us feel safe, but it is also a great source of pleasure. However, life doesn't work that way, and if we depend on having total control, our happiness is bound to become compromised.

This leads me to an important message: Forget about being perfect. Happiness expert Tal Ben-Shahar says there are two categories of people in the world: "Perfectionists" and "Optimalists" (Ben-Shahar, 2009). They sit at opposite ends of the spectrum, and their biggest defining difference is a fear of failure. Perfectionists reject failure and consider it unacceptable. Because of this, they avoid many opportunities and challenges in life. Have you ever not gone for a job because you assumed you'd never get it? Or not attend a class because you were scared you'd look stupid? These are examples of the perfectionist mentality.

Perfectionists are the victims of a fixed mindset. They have an idea of who they are—or who they want to be—and they don't deviate from it. They don't make room for nuance, spontaneity, or ambiguity. Unfortunately, this is the surest way to make yourself miserable because life is complex, and sooner or later, everyone has to face failure of some sort. Optimalists, on the other hand, accept failure. This is not to say that they love failing—no one does—but they accept it as part of the journey and see it ultimately as something to overcome and learn from. This is a feature of a growth mindset.

Perfectionists are also more at risk of developing an ego. If it grows too big, an ego can lead to problems. You risk becoming arrogant in victory and fearful in defeat, neither of which equip you very well for when times get tough. You also measure your value and self-worth by other people's reactions and superficial results. Ego should not be mistaken for pride. Although the two are often closely associated, pride can have many positive connotations. It can be a motivating force for following your dreams, and it can act as an acknowledgment of your effort and merit. Do not be ashamed of feeling proud of yourself. It is a very important aspect of self-love.

If you want to adopt the mindset of a joyful person, work toward becoming an optimalist. Practice having a more positive outlook on life by focusing on benefits instead of faults. James Clear has a quick and easy technique for this. By simply replacing one word in a sentence, you can reframe how you look at a situation. For example, "I *have* to pick up my little brother from school" becomes "I *get* to pick up my little brother from school." Putting a positive spin on things can make even mundane activities seem appealing. Suddenly life is full of opportunities, not burdens.

Become more forgiving and less harsh. Because perfectionists believe that failure is avoidable, they punish it severely whenever they see it. The optimalist will be much more understanding of themselves and others because they know that making mistakes is simply a part of learning and life. Take the approach of the optimalist and be open to suggestions instead of shrinking away from criticism. Be curious about life; the more you say yes, the more opportunities you'll get. In this way, you are far more likely to successfully reach your goals because you won't be hindered by the fear of failure.

Mastering your fears, in general, is an important part of becoming a happier person. You shouldn't feel ashamed for having fears—many of them originate from legitimate reasons. However, fears have a tendency to augment and run havoc in our minds. This is due to the very human condition of imagining the worst-case scenario. Thanks to the evolution of our frontal lobe, we are capable of simulating experiences before we've actually done them. It is an extraordinary feature, but we forget that the simulator is not always right and that it often predicts a bad experience is going to feel much worse than it actually does when we come to it.

Therefore, my advice for overcoming a fear is firstly to talk about it with someone so that it's less "in your head." Nothing destroys a fear faster than being curious about it. The next step is putting yourself in the worst-case scenario, being completely honest, objective, and realistic. Try not to fabricate any unnecessary dramas. Once you've gone through this mental simulation, it might not seem so scary afterward.

Some people take this a step further and go out of their comfort zone to directly face their fear. For example, someone might decide to approach the person they most fear speaking to. Whatever your method is, the main point is not to mistake simulated experiences for objective reality. Once you practice awareness of this, many fears and worries will become demystified.

A final note on the mindset of joyful people is to be proactive. Again, this doesn't mean cramming your day full of extracurricular activities. It means taking responsibility for your choices and actions. Try to avoid thinking things like, "That's just the way it is," as this is a passive attitude that won't get you anywhere.

Being proactive is a good example of when taking ownership is a must. If you are unhappy with your life, focus on the things that you *can* do something about instead. Think about areas where you have influence—your social life, your career, your hobbies, etc. What changes and improvements can you make? Once you realize that you can choose how to live your life, you are on the road to becoming a more empowered, happier person.

Chapter 7: Your Purpose in Life

Wherever you go, go with all your heart... And remember, no matter where you go, there you are. –Confucius

It is a distinctly human quality to think about and plan for the future. We can do this thanks to our frontal lobe: the area of the brain responsible for planning and organizing. These functions allow us to contemplate our lives in a way that no other animal can. While this is a wonderful ability, it also causes us a lot of stress and worry and can lead to the feeling of a lack of purpose in life.

"What is the meaning of life, and where do we fit into it?" is a question that will have as many answers as there are people in this world. It is, therefore, beyond the scope of this book to delve into a philosophical debate here. What *is* necessary is to discuss how having a purpose can directly impact your happiness. We all have those moments in life when we falter and think, "What am I doing here?" Sometimes this is a passing thought or attached to something specific, and other times it is a persistent, nagging feeling about life in general. When we don't know the reasons why we're doing something, we feel uneasy, unsatisfied, and unhappy.

All the evidence points to the fact that people who have a purpose in life enjoy better physical and emotional well-being. In fact, happiness and purpose are so intrinsically linked that they are often used to mean the same thing. This stems from Aristotle's division of happiness into two main categories: *hedonia* and *eudaimonia*. The latter refers to the happiness that arises through a deeper sense of meaning and purpose in your life. It may take more effort to achieve compared to hedonic happiness (fleeting pleasure), but it is deep-rooted and long-lasting. That is why it's so important to find a purpose in life; it not only leads to happiness, but it *is* happiness.

The first step is self-awareness. You must undergo a process of getting to know yourself—something writer Stephen Covey (1989) calls finding your center. Your center is your main source of guidance and motivation in life. It's the element that you look to most for meaning. For example, someone who is family-centered will measure their happiness on the acceptance and approval of their family. They make life decisions based on family models and traditions. Someone who is work-centered, on the other hand, will define themselves by their occupation. They make life decisions based on the needs and expectations of their career.

While there is nothing fundamentally wrong with any of these centers—family, work, spouse, friend, money, self, etc.—none of them are optimal. Covey (1989) notes that we should all strive to be principle-centered instead. This entails identifying your core values and using them as the guiding force behind all of your decisions and actions. Not doing so means running the risk of living your life according to other people's standards and expectations. Only when your core values are satisfied can you lead a meaningful life. Taking the time to think about what really matters to you is, therefore, a crucial step towards finding purpose and achieving happiness. Once you know this, you can make more informed decisions about your life.

When it comes to discovering what matters to you, you might also find it useful to start with the things that you *don't* enjoy doing. What do you really dislike or struggle with? Using a process of elimination, you will quickly narrow down a few areas to focus on. When I feel uncertain about my priorities in life, I lie down or sit somewhere comfortable and quiet. I close my eyes and visualize my future self—five, 15, or even 40 years from now, depending on how far I want to look. I imagine a version of myself that I most want to be. Someone I aspire to. How will that person look, sound, act, even smell? It's exciting.

Next, I imagine myself sitting in front of that older, improved version. I smile at them, and they smile back. Their expression radiates tenderness and wisdom. Then we start to have a conversation. I imagine the questions I would ask: Am I following the right priorities? How could I make you prouder of me? Is there something I should get ready for? Should I spend more time with my parents? I'm very stressed with my job, but I'm afraid to quit—what should I do? And so on.

If you have difficulties finding the answers to these questions, imagine a younger version of yourself instead—perhaps five, 10, or 30 years younger, depending on your age. This should be easier because you know that version of yourself. You can help them by answering any questions they have for you. Using hindsight, you can identify their fears and worries, their hidden passions, and perhaps any misguided priorities. Advise them on what they should do to feel happier and prouder of themselves. You might want to write it all down, and if you find yourself getting emotional, let it happen!

Once you have finished this inspiring conversation and are in a different mental state, you can try the version with your older self again. Let that wiser version of yourself guide you. Be honest, and listen carefully to what is said. Even though it's a hypothetical scenario, subconscious hopes and desires may reveal themselves in your imagination.

To end this chapter, I will share with you another exercise that I found helpful during one of the hardest times in my life. I was at a point where I had no clear purpose, only sadness, and disappointment. I had been pursuing a path that I thought was my dream, but it suddenly closed its doors on me. I will not share the details here as they are not important. What I want to focus on is how I allowed the light to enter my life again.

I remember sitting in my room feeling very melancholic. I was listening to piano music, something I liked to do a lot back then. I took out a blank sheet of paper and asked myself, "If my life was this blank sheet and I could write anything on it, what would I write?" I knew that, deep down, I loved myself and that love has to be proven through loyalty and honesty to your inner self. If I wanted to feel better, then I had to know how to be true to myself. I had to know what it was that I wanted out of my life.

Perhaps this was something I had never shared with anyone. A dream or fantasy I had never talked about. I allowed myself to think about it openly as if there were no consequences or repercussions. I was an innocent child answering a question under the watchful protection of his parents. After some time of thinking, I wrote my answer down.

I allowed myself to envision it for a few minutes before asking another question, one that would change the direction of my life forever: How can I make this happen? The answer was traveling the world, and within two months, I was 11,184 miles (18,000 km) from home, and life wasn't so gloomy anymore. Things had shifted for good.

The exercise I did in my room draws on the technique of envisioning an end goal to help find your purpose. Covey coined this "Begin with the end in mind" (Covey, 1989). By imagining a destination, you get a better idea of the journey you have to take. Similarly, by thinking about what you ultimately want to achieve, you get a better idea of the person you need to be.

So, if you ever feel lost or lacking purpose in your life, ask yourself the same questions I asked. Challenge yourself to be completely honest about what you want out of life. Think about whether you are centered around your own values and principles or someone else's. I should add that there is no rush with this. Give yourself time to figure it out and discover your inner passions. Stay on the alert for hints and clues along the way. And, most importantly, don't wait until you've hit rock bottom to bounce back again.

Chapter 8: Best Practices of Highly Joyful People

Let the beauty of what you love be what you do. –
Rumi

It is my hope that, as you near the end of this book, you have a better idea of how happiness works. In this final chapter, we will take all the ideas that have been discussed so far and put them into actionable practices. Please note: They are not listed in order of importance, and some practices might appeal to you more than others.

There are so many ways to instill positive practices into your life. The following suggestions can be used as a starting point, but if you've been inspired by your own ideas throughout the course of reading this book, I encourage you to go out and implement them as well!

Practice Gratitude

This has been proven to have a marked effect on our physical and mental well-being. Practicing gratitude encourages the brain to look for the positive aspects of life and not just scan for faults. It also gives us a sobering perspective on life. We often take for granted the most basic comforts in life; a roof over our heads, a meal every day, and even access to clean water. When we're having a bad day, practicing gratitude reminds us of the millions of people in the world who are much worse off.

Take the time each day to think about one new thing that you're grateful for. This might be something that happened to you that day or someone who is currently in your life and making you feel good. It might simply be that the sun is shining, and you can see a clear sky. You can keep this as a mental exercise, or you can take it a step further and write your thoughts down. Keeping a gratitude journal is the best way to do this.

As a beginner's challenge, try writing down three new things that you're grateful for each day. Keep it going for 21 days in a row. Afterward, you might find yourself naturally wanting to continue! One of the many benefits of keeping a gratitude journal is that you get to relive all the positive experiences as you write them down. Plus, you then have a collection of happy memories in one place for you to look back on later in life.

Keep a Diary

As well as a gratitude journal, keeping a diary is an excellent way to gather your thoughts and express any concerns or worries. Sometimes referred to as journaling, it is widely recommended by health professionals as a practice for keeping your mental health in check. In his research, psychologist Dan Gilbert has found that writing down the details of a traumatic event significantly helps sufferers of PTSD to recover, both psychologically and physiologically. In some cases, it even generates viral antibodies.

Keeping a diary also allows you to preserve your most important memories. It is often underestimated due to the prevalence of phones and cameras these days. Yes, we can digitally document the events of our lives, but nothing beats recording every little detail of a cherished memory in writing. Details you can't get from a photo. Thoughts and reflections that don't translate through video footage. These little moments become much bigger when we look back on them from the future.

If keeping a diary seems a bit intimidating, try taking the same approach as the gratitude journal. Write just one memory down for each day, perhaps your favorite thing that happened or something that surprised you the most. Another powerful exercise is to write a letter to your future self for you to read in a couple of months, years, or even decades! This allows you to see how your thoughts, worries, and wishes have changed over time, and it can sometimes be a very necessary reminder of how far you have come.

Surround Yourself With the Right People

As we saw in Chapter 4, surrounding yourself with people who love and support you is one of the most important practices for becoming a happier person. This means making an effort to spend quality time with your loved ones. If you rarely see your family or you haven't spoken to a friend in a while, you might want to prioritize communicating with them more. Send them an email, arrange to have a phone call, or meet up with them for a walk or a coffee if it's possible.

The "right people" are the ones you can trust, whom you can laugh with and have deep conversations with. They are the people who listen to you and who are prepared to compromise and apologize when it's needed. The people you should stay away from are the ones who make you feel guilty, anxious, or tired. Even though you might be close with them, it is likely they are having a negative influence on your life. Learning how to set your boundaries with these people and limit your exposure to them is crucial for your well-being.

Spend Time in Nature

It is hard to express just how important it is to spend time in nature. Listing the benefits would be too lengthy here, but it's safe to say that nature has a uniquely restorative and healing effect on the brain and body. It offers the chance to get away from the busyness of life, from the noise and light pollution of cities, and to unplug from all things artificial. It gets us out of the house and exercising, not to mention supplying the simple necessity of fresh air and sunshine, both of which we need to survive. If you don't live in a sunny place, I would recommend making the effort to travel to a place where you get sunshine at least once a year. Sunlight gives us vital energy.

The opportunity to revel in something naturally beautiful is also very soothing for our minds and elevates our moods. You don't have to travel great distances to enjoy nature's benefits either, just going for a lunchtime walk in your local park is beneficial to your health and happiness. Spend some time researching what your area has to offer. Depending on where you live, this could be local nature reserves, lakes, mountain hikes, coastal walks, and so on. If you live in a big city, there is all the more reason to travel to the countryside as you don't get clean, fresh air on a regular basis.

Mindfulness Meditation

Some people might shrink away from this suggestion because they think it involves a lot of training and effort. But a meditation practice can be as simple as closing your eyes and bringing your attention to your breathing for two minutes. It can be savoring each bite of the piece of fruit you are eating or listening to the words exchanged in a conversation. It might just be taking a deep breath of fresh air and feeling it fill and empty your lungs.

Meditation doesn't have to mean stillness, either. You can practice moving meditation through yoga, Pilates, or martial arts like tai chi. And you don't have to do it every day. Once or twice a week will still make a difference to your well-being. The great news is these types of practices have never been more accessible. There are lots of amazing teachers who offer free courses, podcasts, and videos online, so you can spend some time researching what works best for you without having to make a financial commitment.

Mindfulness meditation, in particular, is beneficial because it promotes a focus on the present. It teaches you to be aware of what you're feeling in the moment and to observe your thoughts and senses without judgment or interpretation. You thus become more in tune with your body and can manage your emotions more functionally and helpfully.

It also brings you respite from the hyperreality of society. We live in a noisy, busy world that promotes doing multiple things at once. But mindfulness offers an opportunity for silence and stillness. It promotes enjoyment of the simpler pleasures of life, and if you can take joy in these little things, you will be a much more content person in general.

Practice Generosity

Being generous is not limited to giving money. Giving your time, attention, skills, advice, or any other resource you have is also extremely valuable and can go a long way. The evidence shows that when we engage in acts of kindness, our brain releases oxytocin, which is why giving makes us feel so happy. It explains why joyful people give more.

You may feel that you don't have anything to give, and what you do have, you can't spare. But acts of kindness can be as small as they can be big. To demonstrate this point, here's a challenge for you: After you finish reading this chapter, go to your phone or your computer and send a message to someone in your social circle expressing appreciation for something they have done for you. Notice how heartwarming it feels to acknowledge them. Enjoy imagining their delight—and potential surprise—at receiving a kind message.

If this is not something you usually do, make an effort to practice acts of kindness at least once a week. When we celebrate and appreciate one another, the world becomes a better place. This kind of generosity can be extended to animals and plant life as well. For example, spending time playing with your dog or giving it a massage. Or picking the litter up around a tree or bush and allowing its roots and leaves to breathe. There is nothing more joyous and life-affirming than knowing you have helped someone or something.

Cold Exposure

Exposure to the cold has been championed by Dutch motivational speaker Wim Hof, commonly known as "The Iceman." It is one of three pillars that make up the Wim Hof Method, a set of practices designed to improve all aspects of life, from your immune system, sleep, and hormonal balance, to your stress levels, creativity, focus, and determination.

Cold therapy mostly takes the form of cold showers and ice baths, as these are accessible to all and can be practiced from the convenience of your home. Those who have tried cold therapy have reported a multitude of health benefits, such as increased metabolism, reduced inflammation, swelling, and muscle soreness, improved quality of sleep, higher energy levels, and better focus.

Wim also recommends a series of breathing exercises that hyperoxygenate your body. In a nutshell, this consists of taking 30–40 deep breaths and then holding your breath on the last one for as long as possible. After this, you take one more "recovery breath" and hold for 15 seconds before letting go. The cycle can be repeated 3–4 times.

It is not hard to see how all of these benefits positively impact your happiness. Indeed, many students of the Wim Hof Method swear by its therapeutic effect on depression, anxiety, and other mental health illnesses. Wim Hof himself has used cold therapy to help heal some of the most traumatic wounds a human can endure. His first wife committed suicide when she was only 35, leaving Wim with their four young children. The only way to deal with his grief was to plunge himself into icy cold water, and every day since his wife's death, he has done so.

If you are interested in learning more about the Wim Hof Method, check out his website, where there is a wealth of information and a link to free training videos.

Travel

Traveling to different countries and experiencing different cultures is both inspiring and necessary. It is a chance to get away from work and life, to have fun, to meet new people, and to experience the diversity of the world. It is also deeply fulfilling and leaves one with a sense of a life well lived.

As well as all of the self-serving benefits, traveling promotes a more harmonious and interconnected world. This is because it gives us a healthier perspective on life. The more we are exposed to different cultures and customs, the more easily we can accept that difference is something to be embraced and celebrated, not feared.

We can also more readily seek to understand, inspire, and help other people. This knowledge and experience naturally make us feel happier and more at ease in the world. Narrow-mindedness and ignorance, on the other hand, often warp people's view of the world and lead to feelings of hate, fear, and unhappiness.

I appreciate that traveling can be expensive and inaccessible, but you don't necessarily have to go far to have a different experience. Traveling to a different region or state—or even visiting a nearby town or city you've never been to—might widen your mind. If travel is something you'd like to do more of, try making a conscious effort to save money for trips. Every time you feel like going out for a coffee or buying a new pair of shoes, transfer that money to a savings account instead. At the end of the year, you might find you have enough to finance a weekend getaway or even something longer!

Limit Screen Time

This will hopefully happen naturally once you start picking up some of these practices. Nevertheless, it must be emphasized that limiting screen time will do wonders for your physical and mental well-being. Of course, watching TV or browsing social media can be helpful for unwinding at times, but too much of it is simply mind-numbing. This is especially true if your job requires you to stare at a screen all day. You must give your eyes and brain a break.

Screen time can be replaced by a number of better, healthier alternatives. For example, reading, dancing, playing an instrument or listening to music, arts and crafts, talking with a friend, baking a cake, and so on. And, of course, you could replace your screen time with some of the aforementioned practices, such as meditating, going for walks in nature, or getting involved in community or charity work.

Find Your Strengths

According to psychologist Martin Seligman, the secret to lasting happiness is to find your strengths and know how to apply them (Seligman, 2002). This means finding out what you are naturally good at and choosing a job that plays to those natural abilities. If you can do that, you have found your "calling" and will have a greater sense of achievement and fulfillment in life.

Seligman's research shows that people generally fall into six core values: Courage, Justice, Love, Temperance, Transcendence, and Wisdom. Within each group is a list of signature strengths. To give one example, people who come under the wisdom category have a love for learning and are curious and open-minded. They are street-smart, socially intelligent, and have a better sense of perspective than others. If this is you, you could then take these qualities as a basis for looking at different career options. For instance, you might pursue writing and academia, social work, or go down the international relations and policy-making route.

Whether you find this kind of categorization useful or not, it is certainly smart practice to know your strengths and place yourself in situations where they advantage you. Not only will it make life a bit easier, but it'll also make it more satisfying and rewarding. Happier people choose careers that they enjoy and are good at.

Self-Care

This is just getting a brief mention here, as we discussed in Chapter 2. If you are struggling for inspiration, check out some of the following suggestions. The whole idea is to make time for yourself and the things you love doing.

- Treat yourself to cultural experiences; buy tickets to an art exhibition or music concert.
- Find creative ways to exercise; sign up for a yoga retreat or a dance workshop.
- Go for a walk in nature.

- Go and listen to someone speak publicly who inspires you.
- Attend a spa or go for a massage. Do not just do this once, but go as regularly as possible throughout the year.
- Take a trip to the ocean.
- Go on holiday with a friend.

Laughter

Have you ever heard the saying, "Laughter is the best medicine"? Well, whoever coined it wasn't joking. Laughter can lift you from any mood and make you feel better and more positive within seconds. It is also physically good for you as it exercises muscles in your abdomen. Practice laughter even when times are hard; humor can be a powerful weapon in the darkness. As Charlie Chaplin said, "To truly laugh, you must be able to take your pain and play with it."

Practice Minimalism

Practice being minimal. Truly happy people tend to simplify their lives and steer away from being overly materialistic.

Let Go of the Past

It can be useful to think about the past but do not ruminate on it too much. When you live in the past, you miss out on the present. Feelings of guilt, regret, and revenge are all-consuming and do not make anything better. You will be a much happier person if you can let go of these negative emotions. Accept what has happened, and move on.

Kaizen

I want to end this chapter with the concept of Kaizen. Originating from the Japanese terms for "good change" and "improvement," Kaizen refers to the process of continuous improvement. It was initially adopted by Toyota as a method for improving its manufacturing process, and it has since been used as a business model by a variety of different sectors, from tech companies to healthcare organizations and animation studios. It favors a collaborative approach and encourages people to let go of previous assumptions and look for creative and innovative solutions to problems.

The core belief behind Kaizen is that significant improvements can be achieved through continuous, small, and positive changes. This is the approach I would like you to take to your own personal growth. Think about how Kaizen could be applied to the different aspects of your life—your relationships, health, career, raising children, homemaking, and so on. Focus on adopting practices that are in harmony with Kaizen and impact your life in a solely positive way.

Conclusion: The Happiness Advantage

There is no path to happiness; happiness is the path. – Buddha

Think back to that first question I asked you in the introduction: What does happiness mean to you? Return to those initial notes you made and reflect on what you wrote down. Do you feel differently about anything now? Would you endorse your original associations and requirements for happiness? Perhaps you would, and you stand by everything you wrote, in which case, excellent. Perhaps you have changed your mind about some things, in which case, also excellent.

The task was not about right and wrong. It was for you to compare your understanding of happiness at the time of writing and now. It is my hope that you now have a better idea of what it takes to be truly happy and are better equipped to dismantle the many fallacies that society will throw at you. Most importantly, you should be more able to judge whether the path you are currently on is conducive to inner peace and happiness.

Remember that people who are happy make an effort to be happy. It is not something that you are simply afforded, you have to actively work at it. You have to be aware of your actions and not fall into a mindless routine. You have to reflect on whether your behavior aligns with your core values. And above all, you have to have the courage to change your life if you're not satisfied with it. You must be the advocate of your own happiness.

Because being happy really does put you at an advantage. Put simply, happy people live longer and lead better lives. We all know this to be true, it is an instinctual knowledge we are born with, which is then confirmed by our conditioning. It's the reason why we all chase happiness, why it is the underlying motivation behind everything we do, even when we don't realize it.

And now the science is there to back it up. It has been proven that our brains perform best when they are thinking positively. Our dopamine levels increase, and the learning centers in our brains are optimized. As a result, we do better at school, at work, in our social relationships, and in our ability to navigate life. When we are happy, we have discovered the whole point of living.

Dear Reader

I want to personally thank you for choosing this book from among dozens out there, for acquiring an authorized copy of it and supporting my work, and for making it all the way to the end.

If you liked the content, please consider posting a review or rating on Amazon, it would mean a lot to me and it would help others benefit from my work. It is also the best way to support independent writers like myself.

Thank you.

References

Achor, S. (2011). TEDxBloomington - Shawn Achor - "The Happiness Advantage: Linking Positive Brains to Performance" [YouTube Video]. In *YouTube*. youtube.com/watch?v=GXy__kBVq1M

Ackerman, C. E. (2019, February 16). *What is happiness and why is it important? (+ Definition in Psychology).* PositivePsychology.com. positivepsychology.com/what-is-happiness/

Acosta, K. (2022, March 2). *Here's how much water you should drink a day, according to experts.* Forbes Health. forbes.com/health/body/how-much-water-you-should-drink-per-day/

Better Health Channel. (2012). *Walking for good health.* Vic.gov.au. betterhealth.vic.gov.au/health/healthyliving/walking-for-good-health

Book Review: The Soul of Money by Lynne Twist. (2008, April 4). Citywire.com. citywire.com/funds-insider/news/book-review-the-soul-of-money-by-lynne-twist/a299951

Boucher, D. L. (2023, February 25). Midlife crisis or thriving? Here's what experts say makes midlife more meaningful. *ABC News*. abc.net.au/news/2023-02-26/midlife-crisis-what-is-happiness-and-wellbeing-meaningful-life/102018174

Brooks, D. (2019, May 7). Opinion | The difference between happiness and joy. *The New York Times*. nytimes.com/2019/05/07/opinion/happiness-joy-emotion.html

Cherry, K. (2022, November 7). *How do psychologists define happiness?* Verywell Mind. verywellmind.com/what-is-happiness-4869755

Clear, J. (2014, July 18). *How to build a new habit: This is your strategy guide*. James Clear. jamesclear.com/habit-guide#:~:text=According%20to%20researchers%20at%20Duke

Clear, J. (2018). *Atomic Habits*. Penguin Publishing Group.

Daniel, D. (2021, May). *What is Kaizen (continuous improvement)?* SearchERP.

techtarget.com/searcherp/definition/kaizen-or-continuous-improvement#:~:text=Kaizen%20is%20a%20compound%20of

Fight Mediocrity. (2016, May 27). *How to be happier – Happier by Tal Ben-Shahar, PhD.* youtube.com. youtube.com/watch?v=74Weio-vAZs&ab_channel=FightMediocrity

Gilbert, D. (2007). *Stumbling on Happiness.* Vintage.

Hof, W. (2019). *Welcome to the official Wim Hof method website.* Wimhofmethod.com. wimhofmethod.com/

Hussain, A. (2018). *7 habits of highly effective people [Book summary].* Hubspot.com. blog.hubspot.com/sales/habits-of-highly-effective-people-summary

Joly, J. (2023, February 23). *Which countries have embraced a 4-day workweek and how's it going?* Euronews. euronews.com/next/2023/02/23/the-four-day-week-which-countries-have-embraced-it-and-how-s-it-going-so-far#:~:text=The%20pilot%20in%20the%20UK

Keller, A. (2020, November 9). *Book Review: The Soul of Money by Lynne Twist*. Solopreneur Profit Coach |. atpeacewithmoney.com/2020/book-review-the-soul-of-money-by-lynne-twist/

Lyubomirsky, S. (2007). *Happiness definition | What is happiness*. Greater Good. greatergood.berkeley.edu/topic/happiness/definition

Lyubomirsky, S., Sheldon, K. M., & Schkade, D. (2005). Pursuing happiness: The architecture of sustainable change. *Review of General Psychology*, *9*(2), 111–131. doi.org/10.1037/1089-2680.9.2.111

Memorize Academy. (2017, April 13). *How to be happy [Even if you've forgotten what it feels like]*. youtube.com. youtube.com/watch?v=hsPpaHbvfQs&ab_channel=MemorizeAcademy

Mind. (2020, May). *Sleep and mental health*. mind.org.uk. mind.org.uk/information-support/types-of-mental-health-problems/sleep-problems/about-sleep-and-mental-health/#:~:text=If%20you

Mind Tools Content Team. (n.d.). *MindTools | Home*. mindtools.com.

mindtools.com/a5plzk8/how-to-stop-procrastinating

Mindful Staff. (2021, January 20). *What the Longest Study on Happiness Reveals About Building a Fulfilling Life*. Mindful. mindful.org/what-makes-a-good-life-lessons-from-the-longest-study-on-happiness/

Muelrath, L. (2018, January 26). *Good mood foods: How diet affects happiness - Blue Zones*. Blue Zones. bluezones.com/2018/01/moods-and-foods/#:~:text=Research%20tells%20us%20that%20plant

O'Connor, A. (2021, May 6). How food may improve your mood. *The New York Times*. nytimes.com/2021/05/06/well/eat/mental-health-food.html

Practical Psychology. (2016, June 26). *How to be happy - The secret of authentic happiness - Martin Seligman*. youtube.com. youtube.com/watch?v=Mp8xN1K-ITs&ab_channel=PracticalPsychology

Suliman, A. (2023, March 8). Can money buy happiness? Scientists say it can. *Washington Post*.

washingtonpost.com/business/2023/03/08/money-wealth-happiness-study/

TED Talks. (2012, April 26). *The surprising science of happiness | Dan Gilbert*. youtube.com. youtube.com/watch?v=4q1dgn_C0AU&ab_channel=TED

Twist, L. (2017). *The soul of money: Transforming your relationship with money and life*. W. W. Norton & Company.

Vargas, R. A. (2023, January 26). World's oldest person on the keys to longevity: "stay away from toxic people." *The Guardian*. theguardian.com/us-news/2023/jan/26/worlds-oldest-person-115-maria-branyas-morera-california

Wai Yan Tun, K. (2021, October 22). *Summary: Master your time, master your life by Brian Tracy*. Waiyancan.com. waiyancan.com/summary-master-your-time-master-your-life-by-brian-tracy/

Waldinger, M. S. & R. (2023, January 13). *The good life: Lessons from the world's longest scientific study of happiness*. Next Big Idea Club. nextbigideaclub.com/magazine/good-life-lessons-worlds-longest-scientific-study-happiness-bookbite/38955/

Waldinger, R., & Schulz, M. (2023). *The good life.* Simon & Schuster.

Walker, M. P. (2017). *Why we sleep : unlocking the power of sleep and dreams.* Scribner, An Imprint Of Simon & Schuster, Inc.

Made in United States
Troutdale, OR
10/27/2024

24172941R00053